SABRINA CARTWRIGHT

From There To Here

Collection From 2010 to Present Day

Contents

From There To Here The Meaning Of

This book is a collection of my favorite poems from my first three poetry collections, Inside This Crazy Head of Mine, Words To The Forgotten, and Privately Owned and operated. It shows the growth that I have made in not just my writing style but my personal life as well, I have been through absolute hell and back the last ten years and on this journey, I have met so many wonderful people, learned new things, experienced heartbreak, rage, everything in between. Now going forward, with the last ten years of my life behind me I finally have a general idea of the path ahead of me. Some details I won't ever know until I get there but just knowing that there is a divine and beautiful reason for me being here and sharing my pain and my work as I learn and grow will be an amazing thing to continue to fight for. To me, the meaning of the title "From there to here" is a celebration of all that I have overcome so far. There is still more work to be done but the work I have done so far deserves to be acknowledged and celebrated, even if others don't quite understand how much mental trauma I had to go through to get to where I am today. The fact that I never even thought I would make it this far and that I am still here and doing my best to create a life for myself is surprising every day that I wake up.

I think back to myself from a year ago and I barely even recognize myself. I've been making moves that I five years ago would never have dreamt I would be making, taking chances slowly here and there. Slowly letting go of the pain from the past knowing I have the brightest future ahead of me, and I never would be here now if two years ago I didn't start making the choices that I did. Things are still weird and confusing right now, but I know if I just keep going I will get to where I want to be.

I Wonder

I'm a little adventurous
   Some may say that I am obnoxious
   All I am is who I want to be
And I guess what I am is a dream

But who are you to judge what I do
   They think I don't have scars buried too?
   But I'm only human
   And humans make mistakes
   My past isn't what there is to blame

I wonder why I am here at times
   I'm waiting for the world to tell me why
   Do I have a story to tell?
   All I do is sit and dwell
   Is my story over yet?
   I can't wait on the sun to set

Why do people judge what you do
   They think that they are perfect too
   Everyone's human and
   Humans make mistakes
   Our past are never the ones to blame
   Just the voices that drive us insane

At 2 am when you can't sleep
   Tossing and turning but can't breathe
   Life feels suffocating
   And I know it can be heartbreaking
   I don't want to be broken
   So many words left unspoken

I won't judge for what you do
   I know you're just human too
   Humans make mistakes
   They bury their scars
   You should be known for what you are

Broken Bird

B roken bird don't clip your wings
    You'll learn to fly again
    All on your own
No push and no shove
Broken bird it's all up to you
I know that you know what to do

Give your wings a chance to heal
    You'll forgive and forget
    And it will be real
    Broken bird it's not over quite yet
    There's a lover you haven't yet met

Your voice is cracking
    And you can't find the strength to move on
    But broken bird you know the song
    The words may not come out

Broken bird don't close your mouth

Give your wings a chance to heal
   Forgive and forget let it be real
   Broken bird it's not over yet
   There's a lover you haven't yet met

Your sparkle he won't dull
   There's so much for you to learn
   Hold on please still
   Broken bird it's not over yet
   There's a lover you haven't yet met

Give your wings a chance to heal
   Forgive and forget
   His love was never real
   Broken bird life isn't over yet
   There's a lover you haven't yet met

I Can Sense It

I can sense it
    When someone starts
    To lose interest in me
It's so easy to figure out
The conversations become dull
The light in their eyes fades away
I overthink every possible
Scenario of why this could be happening
Because it always does
Usually they find someone
Better than I
Someone that can give them
What they desire
Someone more confident and prettier
Than I
I can easily take a hint
Even though I prefer an explanation
But an explanation is never what I receive

Because they think it's easier to just walk away
Then to let me know
That I am not what they want anymore
It scares me
And I hate getting close to people
And opening up
Because they can leave with all my fears
Whenever they so desire too
I over think the silence
When in fact it's nothing
It drives them away
They say all the right things
That get my heart racing
And I believe they won't leave
But they do
And it always catches me by surprise
Even though I know I seen it coming
It still hurts
Then I spend forever trying to forget them
Until the next one comes along
And I take a chance
And let them in

You can dance with your demons, I made a home at rock bottom

Y ou threw me down to rock bottom,
    Thinking I'd lay down and let you win,
    thought I'd let you get away with the damaged caused
Assumed I'd retaliate and cause a riot
But I built a home down there,
I became friends with my shadow while you still battle with
yours
    While I walked around on eggshells trying not to anger
The monster within you
You danced freely and laughed as I walked away
Thinking you had won and I'd come back for more
But no,
The window shattering scream I let out
Freed myself and from your grasp
Don't think I don't know what your intentions were
Because I may be quiet, and I may be polite

But I am not stupid and I'm not afraid to release
What I've been holding back
You on the other hand, don't care who you hurt
As long you look innocent in the end
Your minions will figure it out in time
Until then, I will walk with my head held high
Letting the damage within you
Dance with the devil

Your Shoe is Untied

"Your shoe is untied" They say to me
  I look down, at the loose thread
  And in face it is

"Aren't you going to tie it?" They ask,
  I scrunch my shoulders
  And feel the world watching me

"Probably not right now." I say,
  Feeling the entire weight of the world
  Bearing its teeth on my body

"You're going to trip,
  and you're going to fall." They warn me,
  and I know that but I don't care

"Okay then weirdo." They laugh
  And I stand and stiffen a smile

As their shirt is inside out

Depression

Depression is a strange creature, It twists and turns your insides out. Makes all what was good, So full of doubt. It eats away at everything you've known and loved, All those happy feelings start to push and shove. Depression can leave you feeling hopeless, All the feeling you've known joyless. Everything you've once loved has turned to hate, You've just begun to accept this horrible fate.

What depression is to me is like a long narrow bridge, Going across the world and sinking into a deep hole. It starts off very clear and you can see as to where you are going, And then out of no where you start twisting into a fog. That fog becomes all that you see, And all that you know. You know nothing other then that dark twisted cloud, Its more then you will ever allow.

Once your life has been taken over by this dark fate, You start to spiral out of control and maybe its too late. You feel that the world is crashing down, All those voices just get so loud.

Everything is your fault that's what you feel, Everything you touch is just so unreal. Even the pain makes you feel numb,

Like a monster that is becoming a phantom.

Depression is a feeling so left unnamed, Feels like everyday you are going insane. You hear those voices inside your mind, Nothing you do can make you unwind.

Hurting more and more every day, No one listens to a word you say. All I know is the darkness will turn to light, All the wrong may become right.

Good/Bad/Days/Weeks/Month-s/Years

❦

The good days are good
  And the bad days are worse
  The good days I survive
Even though it all hurts
I get up pretty early
Leave the house in a hurry
But the back of my mind
Won't begin to unwind
The good days I can't stop talking
I wind myself up on coffee
But when I crash
I crash down pretty hard
The bad days last for weeks
A hole dug way too deep
I lay for hours in my bed
Replaying nonsense words

That has been said
Even though things feel good
A single touch of chaos can turn them bad
There's not much that makes me sad
Even being left on read from a boy
The shit I do during my good days
Comes back to haunt me on the bad days
The energy on the good days
Gives me confidence to do and say what I can't
On the bad days
The bad days are a storm that leave a mess for the good days
To clean up after its wake
I can't figure out how more of it I can take
The good days I don't take advantage
Because it's usually just one day at a time
All I want is less bad days
But it's so hard to try

Crossing the Street

Anxiety is like crossing the street
       You want to go
       And everyone around you is telling you
Just cross the damn street
But your legs just won't cooperate
You don't want to get hit
But you know you need to get
To the other side of that road
Depression is seeing a busy street
And not truly caring weather you get hit or not
Like go ahead what do I have to lose?
Anxiety and depression is walking halfway because you don't
care
But stopping because you're actually scared

I Wonder

& I wonder if she ever comes up behind you

To hug you while you're cooking pasta as I did on the very first day you took me home

Played two notes of a song that I hear on the radio constantly, my socks were soaked from the snow that cascaded down that night

& We ran for the bus and almost missed it, I was out of breath but the running isn't what did it

Sometimes I question if you even existed or it was my imagination that any of that ever occurred, these things don't happen in anything other than a movie, but now we have a soundtrack that plays in the background as time brings us closer to each other, please don't dance with someone else... Energetically I am yours but in reality, it's coming close Do I have to say your name so you know this piece is written about you?

its like I don't exist to you anymore

Why I write

I write because I have a voice
    A voice that is too scared to come out on its own
    A voice that has so much to say
But can't find the courage to say it out loud
I write because it's easier for me to put what I am thinking
Into actual words
Because speaking means stumbling and fumbling around
Watching the crowd
And all of their little mannerisms
And coughs and stares
And wondering if I will say something wrong
Or I will stop speaking in the middle of a sentence
I have the power of words in my voice
I have so many lessons to teach
I write because I am afraid
I am afraid of the words not coming out
The way I want it to be told
I write because

I have so many stories to tell
So many things that float around inside my head
I love every second of writing
I love the late nights
The coffee jitters
The unanswered text messages
And busy days
Writing has always been my voice
And will continue to be my voice
Maybe one day
My writing will be a story
Passed down from generations
And years from now
Everyone will know of all the stories I have told
Maybe one day
My voice will change lives
And have an impact on the world
Or maybe
My writing will just be words
Left unread on the page
Just waiting to be opened
Who knows
All I know
Is I am going to keep on writing
And telling the world my story

The Lies, The Truth and More

How long must I blame myself,
The truth was not my fault.
The lies is what I hide,
The hurt is what everyone sees.
The city burns at the sight of life,
It bleeds in the pit of darkness.
It's not okay, to keep this
Away from my soul
To not make sense of love and life,
Where are the flames when I need them
I need them so bad
I'm not going to watch you destroy it all
I'm not going to let myself fall
Where did the missing go
They ventured so far
So far to become one
And now
Nothing lies between

19

Paper Roses

You give me a bouquet of paper roses,
I trace the paper in my hand
And it falls apart
Just as easily as you left me.
I set them on fire,
It ignites just as easily as the fire
You started in my chest
I throw it on the ground,
Just as you have done to me
I stomp on it and walk away
Just like you walked away from me
Now the paper roses and I
Are just ashes in the sky
And I'll never know why

Long Distance

You showed me your guitars& Your small little
apartment
You're so far away now and I hate it
I can't do anything to bring you closer
To where I am
And I can't turn back time
to make you stay
Stay here with me

I want this crazy
misunderstood whatever this is
I want us to grow I don't care the distance
Across the street
Or across the country
Stay with me
I'd rather have this
Crazy messed up relationship
Then something easy and

perfect and right beside me

Skype dates and staying up
  late 3 am for me and midnight for you
  You're the choice I'll always choose
  Even when I have to be up soon
  Time zones and long distance calls
  I want this over nothing at all
  I want this crazy misunderstood
  whatever this isI want us to grow
  I don't care the distance
  Across the street
  Or across the country
  Stay with me
  I'd rather have this
  Crazy messed up relationship
  Then something easy and
  perfect and right beside me

They tell me to give up
  They tell me to forget you
  Because I deserve better
  But I don't want better
  I don't want someone here
  Because they aren't you
  All I want is you

I want this crazy
  misunderstood whatever this is
  I want us to grow I don't care the distance
  Across the street

Or across the country
Stay with me
I'd rather have this
Crazy messed up relationship
Then something easy and
perfect and right beside me

Reasons To Hold On

here may be reasons to let go of this life and what it has
to offer,
     Yet so many reasons to hold on and not to suffer.
One reason to hold on would be for the life I want to live,
And for the things I have to give.
A smile to pass on to everyone who needs,
And to continue doing the things in life that I please.
Another would be to watch the sun set down at night,
And the leaves change color falling from their heights.
As well as to watch my friends laugh from a distance,
Their smiles gazing down and eyes all glistened.
I may have days where I want my story to end,
But I also have days where their is a life I have to defend.

Not Cinderella

You are prince charming
But I am not Cinderella
I won't be waiting until midnight
For everything to return to normal
It already is
You won't be sweeping me off my feet
I'm already on the ground
And you're off living your dreams
I'm here alone
Waiting for you to realize
When will you realize?
I'm sorry I'm not Cinderella
And I can't make you fall in love with me
At midnight
Or ever

Discovering

Discovering the meaning of what I am worth,
Trying to overcome the pain and the hurt.
Not letting voices inside my mind,
Leaving negative thoughts behind.
I stop and think to explore the day,
I start to realize what I can change.
I know I am so much more than what I think,
Life passes by so fast its hard to even blink.
Felt like falling into a pit of despair,
Days of happiness had felt so rare.
Time to make effort in all that I do,
Cannot let life once again come unglued.

Home In The Cold

W alking in the cold,
　　　Going no where but home.
　　　Stranded in this deserted maze,
Just trying to find my place.
My hands reaching the point of numbing,
but I'm on my way, so I'll keep on walking.
Amazed by how good I'm doing,
but my thoughts are whats troubling.
Can't seem to control my mind,
fear and hope don't seem to combine.
Why wasn't I paying attention,
is that what was mentioned?
On the point of breaking down,
swimming in the tears that I surround.
But as I reach close to my destination,
all I feel is this depression.
I don't want to walk in this door,
Cause I don't want to hear this no more.

My scars that I have will never seem to fade,
They worsen even more each day.
Keeping up a steady pace,
All I want is to give up the chase.
This won't help the hurting,
and I will keep up struggling.
Now I'm finally home,
Because I got no where else to go.
But if I had the chance,
I would run as fast as I can.

Snowy Kisses

When the snow falls
　　From the sky
　　　it takes me back
to that night we first met
I still get that feeling
3 years later even

We walked and we talked
　And I wasn't cold
　You pushed me into the snow
　And I never wanted to go
　You walked me home
　And that night I knew
　It would be you
　It's still you

Coffee dates and snowy kisses
　Three years later and I still miss this

Spending an entire day alone with you
Even when outside a storm brews
I don't know how to move on
Even so long after you're gone

We walked and we talked
    And I wasn't cold
    You pushed me into the snow
    And I never wanted to go
    You walked me home
    And that night I knew
    It would be you
    It's still you

I should forget you
    And in the summer months I do
    But when the snow falls
    It takes me back to you
    And the night we first met

We walked and we talked
    And I wasn't cold
    You pushed me into the snow
    And I never wanted to go
    You walked me home
    And that night I knew
    It would be you
    It's still you

Silent Disruptive Lover

Y our all that matters to me now,
    I won't give up on you somehow.

When I have you I can't think,
I feel so great my mind starts to sink.

You're not supposed to be with me,
   Or anywhere near at all.

And when your around me,
   I cannot help but fall.

I can't help but wonder if, this is an addiction,
   or lust.
   I always gotta have you,
   That I must.

You make me so messed up,

And you could ruin my life.
But if I don't have you,
My heart it will bust.

6:30 Am Coffee

My alarm is set for 6:30
But my mind won't let me sleep
Too many thoughts on a war inside my brain
Only raging for their own personal gain
I'll probably press snooze when the alarm
Screams and I'll be bearly awake

Tomorrow I'll need a large cup of coffee
And you and I still won't be talking
Heartbreak floods into the next day
You won't listen to any words I say

After my day is over
I'll head on home into my bed
Close my eyes for a long nap
And the night before will replay
And I'll set my alarm for 6:30
The cycle will repeat

Until you say sorry to me

Tomorrow I don't even want coffee
    Because you and I still aren't talking
    And I'm still mad but it reminds me
    Of sitting with you alone
    Now I'm screaming into the void

6:30 am comes too soon,
    I'm so sick of pressing snooze
    I don't want to get up at all
    I'll wait around all day for your call

You finally text me to meet me over coffee
    Maybe then we can just start talking
    I'm not mad anymore
    I just want you back at my door

The Mission

I am not lost, nor am I confused.
  For I am searching for a meaning here,
  I am searching for my soul.
I discarded it long ago,
Now it is my mission to receive.
I know the mission is dangerous,
But I shall succeed in finding myself once more.
The nights will be followed by terror,
And days will stand still where ever they begin
I won't be scared when I find it,
I won't want to turn back when I get closer.
The risks are not limited, the doors
Won't shut at all
I know where I am going,
And what I am after.

I Miss You

I   miss you
     But what does that even mean
     Do I miss you being around?
Or miss your voice?
What do I miss most about you?
Your smile?
Maybe it's your laugh,
And your hands,
And your mouth
And everything in between
Does I miss you mean I want you here?
Of course it does
But you can't just show up here
I get that
And I'll be okay without you for now
But you're the missing piece that makes
Me feel whole again

Words To The Forgotten

So many have passed through my life,
   So many have left scars with their knives,
   So many have loved and left
These are the words to the forgotten
This is my pick up where I got broken hearted
Things may never go back to what they where
Because all in the past is such a blur
I have to teach myself to be okay
I have to move on and pretend everyday
It's hard and it feels wrong
But I'll be alright

Because I know I am strong

These words to the forgotten, they are my heart and my soul.
They are everything I went through spilled out onto the pages.
My very brain is what you are experiencing here, even more
deeper than "inside this crazy head of mine." I will not hold

back on anything I feel or experience. I just want my world out there, for the real world to experience fully. It doesn't matter what I make, or what I gain from publishing my life and my thoughts; what matters is what you gain from reading my words and knowing my struggle and my gains and losses. I am vulnerably letting everything go, and I have no ounce of regret doing so.

-S.C

Stop Lights

S top light says red;
yet i continue to go
racing through the stop sign too
on my way to you

I don't listen
and I never do
that's why my heart
doesn't know what to do

warning signs in my vision
I just want to win this
but you're the only sign
stuck in my head

another red light;
here we go again

I'm The One Who Left

I'm the one who left
    Because I didn't know you
    Wanted me to stay
But I packed my bags anyway
And went so far away

and you moved on
    And forgot all about me
    And I'm the one whose here alone
    and I just want to jump on a plane home

But what's the point in that?
    When you won't want me back
    and you'll forget all about us
    And our memories

I have to be okay with that
    Because I'm the one who left

I'm The One Who Left

And I know you won't wait
It's only been a week and you've already
Found somebody else to call your own
And I'm out here all on my own

Blank Canvas

every morning; you are an empty page. & i don't know how to fill in the pages of us. i try to fill it with brightness/ with color and happy voices; but as the day wears on, and I wear down. it still remains empty; as I don't know what to say to you. there's no dialogue, there's just a white blank canvas.

Not Alone

Y ou,
  reading this right now
  breathe for a moment
and look around
it may be dark
or it may be light
and the room your in
may be surrounded by people
but you still feel alone

you are not alone;
  you have these words
  to keep you company
  and guide you
  where ever it is you go next

maybe we don't
  know each other yet

but I am your friend
I've survived through it all
as well as you

so keep on reading;
and keep on breathing;

Remain; Mutual With Myself

i can feel it in my chest
    i can feel it in my thighs
    i don't want to feel it
guess i gotta get high
don't want to go back
to the surface where - it started from
i just want to remain ; mutual with myself

guess i gotta ; get back to what
    i used to before you
    decided to cross
    my very path in front of me ;
    and walked out that very door

Silence Isn't Quiet

S ilence isn't quiet
in fact; its louder than any sound
that can be heard for miles
silence is deafening
when you walk into a room
and the person you love
doesn't say a word
and you're left feeling
stupid and absurd

Quit Punching Walls

I know when you're mad
 I can see it all over your face
 You try to hide it
But I see right through you
All I want to do is hold you
But I know it's not the best thing
To do
Because you take it out on
Everything that you choose
It's kind of terrifying
And I stay out of the way
Almost all day
Even if I know I didn't do anything wrong
It feels like I did
I don't like it when you're mad
The doors you kick
And words you scream
I'm sorry If I did anything

to set you off
I never meant to
And I'll leave you alone

Used To Be

I guess I hope too much
    Maybe I set my expectations
    Way too high
Maybe there's less of a future
Behind all of these lies

Everything was so perfect, perfect
    But it was just a fantasy, fantasy
    Now I'm just lonely, and hoping
    Things will get back to
    The way they used to be, used to be

Moments became hours
    Which turned into days
    And then into weeks and
    Months and years
    But where do I go now
    After all of these tears

Everything was so perfect, perfect
   But it was just a fantasy, fantasy
   Now I'm just lonely, and hoping
   Things will get back to
   The way they used to be, used to be

September, will be here soon
   Then October comes around next
   The years almost over
   But I can't help but
   Want to go back,
   Want to go back

Everything was so perfect, perfect
   But it was just a fantasy, fantasy
   Now I'm just lonely, and hoping
   Things will get back to
   The way they used to be, used to be

Blanket of Doom

I have to force myself to get out of bed in the morning
     To tell myself there's things that need to get done
     And schedules to follow
But my mind won't allow me to fully wake
Even coffee can't keep me going 100%
And lying in bed all day leaves me with regret
Because there's thing I should be doing
And places I should be going
But my bed I continue to lay
Without my minds say

Shopping with Anxiety

I wander aimlessly around the store
    I'm not even sure what for
    I'm terribly anxious and I can feel myself shake
Someone walks up and asks "how can I help you today?
I say, I'm just browsing but thanks
I continue my search
For absolutely nothing
Then I remember while I'm down the cereal isle
That I came here for milk
But milk I can't seem to find
Even though there's so many signs
But I'd rather wander around aimlessly
Then to ask for help
Because that's less revolting then being told
That the milk is right in front of my face

I am Anxiety

I am a storm
   Filled with hurricanes and rain
   Thunder and hail
It comes down on the world
Faster than an oncoming train

I am a hurricane
  Tearing down everything in my wake
  Days I don't care who I hurt
  Because to me its what they deserve

I am the dark clouds
  Flying over your city
  and scaring everyone
  letting them think their world is ending

I am the tightness in your chest

When you can't breathe
Because I am anxiety - S.C

Slow & Steady

───⟨ ❧ ⟩───

When the shadows come flying through
And your heart is black and blue
May your demons be laid to rest
And your sorrows build its nest
Let the morning rise when it's ready
And your heartbeat becomes steady
It's going to be alright in the end
Love is another word to bend
Create your new day when you wake
Forget the sorrows from yesterday
The sun will rise when it's ready
Let your heartbeat slow and steady
-S.C

A new world

When i'm writing
i'm creating another world
one to come up with
anything my mind can process
anything i want will come to life
i am not alone
when i write
because my characters are there with me
it may seem psychotic but
they are my friends
and i create life for them
and a life with them

Heart On Fire

You're a storm
  I'll be your rain
   Call me your thunder
I'll drown out all your pain

Call me a lover
 Or call me a fighter
 But I won't give in
 To my heart on fire

The walls may fall down
 But I won't let you in
 Unless you tell me my secrets
 I told you to forget
 Don't make me regret

Call me a lover
 Or call me a fighter

But I won't give in
To my heart on fire

Truly Awake

My strength comes from within me
I don't need anyone to try and fix me
When I was never broken to begin with
Tormented by demons that were
Actually angels wanting to send a message
That I could never truly listen to
I breathe life into the day
When I truly become awake

Crossing The Street With Anxiety

The sign says go;
    you know that walk sign
    that indicates
that it is safe
but you're trapped in a mind that tells you
it's not safe; don't go yet
but the people in the cars
they look at you
like you are crazy;
maybe you are crazy
because your feet won't let you just go
now it's too late
and the sign has gone red
and the people inside their cars
they just shake their heads
then there's a voice
trapped inside your mind
"What have you got to lose?"

"Nobody will miss you!"
so you take that step to cross
all senses of reality have been lost
so there you are;
in the middle of the road
and you still feel all alone
but they honk and set your mind straight
you wake up from the daze
and continue running on through
realizing how close that was
and look back to mistake
that could have been avoided
if you had crossed the street
in the first place

Toxic Mix

We are a toxic mix
You have it all figured out
And I have yet to wake up in the morning
And have the desire to make it happen
You want things that I can't give
Your kiss is like poison
But keeps me coming back for more
Like an addiction that I can't detox from
I met you
And my entire world changed right before my eyes
I thought before I knew you
Miracles like this only happen in movies
But it takes time to let this reality sink in
My heart can't take another break
So it pushes you away
Hoping you'll run back to me
And forget how bad we are for each other
Because being together is what is right

Women Should SUPPORT Each Other!

W oman shouldn't be talking negatively about each other. Especially after a break up and the other one has moved on, you see them out and about with their new significant other and you think to yourself.

"Wow she's such a downgrade compared to me." or "im such an upgrade compared to her"

Its so easy to compare yourself to another woman, especially in that type of situation. But in reality, that type of behavior is so damn toxic it implies that you believe you're better than the other woman. We should be uplifting each other instead of comparing each other. Or at the bar in the bathroom and you judge another woman's sleazy outfit, even me saying that is toxic enough and it's something we don't realize we are doing. It's her body and she can wear whatever makes her comfortable on a night out.

If a woman decides to sleep around that's her choice, it doesn't make her a slut or anything just means she is using her body how she decides to. Her body and her rules. And if a woman decides not to sleep around, doesn't at all make her at all a prude. Again, her body and her rules. Respect it or leave her alone.

Its so easy to get caught up in media's expectations of who we are supposed to be, but that doesn't mean we have to practice that philosophy. It's our lives and we can choose what and what not to do without anyone approval or disapproval. As woman we need to work together and lift each other up instead of dragging each other down.

Spreading gossip and lies about someone doesn't get you very far either, it's so easy to get caught up in that but it's also just as easy to not give in to that type of temptation.

Its a beautiful short life and we need to enjoy every moment of it all, and not get dragged down into the flames of society's expectations.

-S.C

My Brain Has Too Many Tabs Open

My brain is like the internet,
    with a million tabs open
      tons on the go
bouncing between so many options
there's random music playing somewhere
just can't find it
try dealing with this
all day
everyday
3 am
5 pm
when im sleeping
when im eating
everyday i'm breathing
I can't seem to close them
ctrl/alt/delete
doesn't ever do anything
its only a matter of time

before too many open
and they decide to just crash

Chapter 43

Throw me a pity party
    with balloons and streamers
    and maybe some cake
I'll probably be late but ill be there
feel sorry for me when i tell you the story of my life
I only want your mascara tears, and sniffy noses
and "I'm sorry that happen to you"
i'll pretend its a surprise
but I seen it coming
or is this an intervention?
maybe even a lesson
that's okay
ill be the only one there
alone at my own pity party
bring some alcohol please
we can all take shots at how much i suck
i'll invite my bullies
they'll only be there for the free booze and cake

but that's okay
least i won't be alone
at this pity party of fake friends and lovers /

you can leave/ whenever you please / i can handle the rejection
/ just trying to fake it to perfection / what did you bring for
a present? / oh, the present isn't for me? / then what are you
doing here? / please leave
    I'm only kidding/ i don't want to be alone / home is where I
don't / want to go / that's where I'll throw my own pity party /
and it will be sad and Grey / don't worry /
    there will be another pity party in a few days - S.C

Didn't Need To Yell

y ou didn't need to yell
& make me feel so low
in such a vulnerable moment
of mine
what I did wasn't meant
and I don't know how many times
i can say sorry
obviously nothing i do or say
can make this right again
-S.C

Privately Owned And Operated

all my life, I've told the same story. I told a story of abuse, low self-esteem, my power being taken from me, growing up with a broken family, heartbreak, illness, depression, anxiety, feeling misunderstood, lack of control and so much more.

I am here to retell my story; I am here to reinvent myself. to tell of a new tale, one of compassion, strength, a fight that's inside that is only fueled with the pain of what was and what will never be ever again.

a fight so strenuous that I've almost called it quits; a fight that left me feeling so alone and powerless; until one day when I had enough and decided to take it all back to slowly begin rebuilding my life from scratch and putting the pieces together one by one;

This is me, taking ownership of my life and freeing myself from the chains that hid me away, the way of life that I never wanted to live and becoming the woman I am meant to be but honoring the sweet little girl that was so happy and full of magic.

the two previous books were my old story;
   here's to a brand new beginning.

Play It Safe

No longer do I desire to play it safe,
    Even if the ground cuts my feet
    What I desire is to run free,
And make memories with myself
Have fun, laughter and live among the trees
Dance in the moonlight, as it shines down
Sleep under the stars, find my soul
Find the truest me
Walk barefoot on the earth
With the soil beneath me,
welcoming me home
to where I truly belong
And destroy society's expectations of success
Because success is internal
Freedom is my success

Healing

Healing.

A word I've used over and over the last year and a half. The process of which an individual takes the time they need to discover themselves and the world around them. Lot of which happened to me over the many previous years of life on this earth. Many moments in solitude, seeking answers and higher truth. A lot of comparisons of other people's lives, and lying to myself about situations that from other people's point of view don't seem that bad but from mine has been horrendous and my story deserves to be told. Just as many other stories of other people deserve to be told.

But I....am different, because my perception of the world has always been different from others, and maybe I am not where everyone else thought me to be. But, I am where I am supposed to be and that in itself is a beautiful selfless journey.

Many days, nights, weeks, months of second-guessing myself and my emotions and realizing I am exactly where I am meant to be on this earth and in this moment my mind, my heart, and soul are being merged into one being. My past self, my present self, and my future self are all fighting against each other. Arguing about which way to go, fighting with my mind especially when those who have said they will always support me turn their back when I'm aching to pave my own way. The honesty and authenticity I've had to have with myself as I fight my way through this mess I have created, fighting with the voices that are holding me back saying I should be doing something more to contribute to this world, that what I am doing is not enough but it is so much more than enough. Just because someone has it worse than you doesn't mean your story isn't important, or that you aren't allowed to tell your story the way you've experienced it. People only know you based on what they've experienced with you.

Craving solitude all the time is the most freeing way of listening to my true self come through, I decide to be alone until I ache for the warm touch of a friend. But I still stay away because I know this time is necessary for me to trudge forward in life. Even though two years have passed it just feels like its all happening simultaneously. I am not the same woman I was when I started this journey, this is just the beginning there is so much more work to be done and many more adventures to embark on.

Some of the things I've discovered about myself the last few years have truly shocked even myself, and some of the people closest to me. Its like I've kept the true me hidden out of fear the people I love the most wont accept me for who I am, and they will only continue to view me from their own perspectives. But I realized along the way that this was only causing more damage and hurt on my behalf. The intention was never to push people away but to distance myself so much until I come to the realization that healing was never gathering up new things about myself, but discarding things about myself that were not true. And not seeing things out of the lens of other people who think they know me better than I do, because I've only begun to scratch the surface. There's many more layers of me to get to know, and I will stop at nothing to find the real me.

Point Of View

Y ou weren't seeing things
     from my point of view, you were on the outside
     looking in,
and that itself distorted your perception into
something that isn't me
And upon accepting that
I will be set free

Stupid Little Dreamer

I 've been called most of my time on earth
   Staring off into space not understanding
   Why the world was just so cruel
Where else would I spend my time
When my reality is unsafe
I have one foot in my own little heaven
And another in this place we call "real life"
But, Yet they never asked me
what I was dreaming about
They only laughed and laughed
Said my thoughts were stupid
Get your head out of the clouds
your dreams are unattainable
And I would never reach them
What they didn't know is that I was dreaming
Of a better tomorrow for everyone
Not just for myself
One filled with laughter and love

And joy and happiness
A tomorrow in which dreams are attainable
No matter how "unrealistic" they seemed to be
That stupid little daydreamer will one day be
Someone they never thought I would be

I Think I Fall

I think I fall in love with anyone
   That I connect with on a soul level
   It's not romantic kind of love
But the type you never forget
The type that accidentally bumping into them
Years later when the thought of them has passed
Makes you get that warm fuzzy feeling
That you had when you first met them
The type of unconditional love that allows you to
Support them on their journey
Knowing you crossed paths with them for a reason
Even if you don't know it then
You may find out years from now on a warm
Tuesday afternoon when the phone rings
And they share the best news ever
You smile, grateful to have met them at all
And wish them well as they follow their dreams

Old Me Was Blocked Like A Beaver Damm

Old me was like a beaver dam,
    so many blockages where the words did not flow
    New me, lets all the emotions out
a warrior waiting to fight
the dam breaks and the words do not stop
All-day every day my soul speaks to me
Old me would ignore it, call it silly
but now I know what it is
So beyond the stubbornness old me carried
Perhaps new me will finally listen
& Let my words flow to the pages
and the souls meant to read them

Can't Always Control The Weather

accepting where I've been
  even if it's not where I wanted to be
  all of the people I had to meet
where on that path for the desired reason
everything leading to the other and
then to something more
makes the path appear weathered and torn
but brighter days ahead
need repetition in our heads
taking a few days, weeks, months to feel alive
is better than fighting to try and survive
starting tasks without following through
is something that I had always seemed to do
it's frustrating because those are the things I want
but always did what I had to do
because what I truly wanted went against the grain
And I become fearful and hide away until I feel okay again
I know it won't be this way forever

but you can't always control the weather

Standing Up Felt Wrong

d ay after day
    I begin to pray
    and I wonder,
am I doing enough?
For the world to pave the way
away different than most
because the opposite makes me bored
but I need to contribute in some way
in order to survive this crazy world
but I can't just sit around waiting
for life to bring me joy
when the joy that I need is literally right
in front of me
But I feel so lost at times
fearful of the consequences on their way to me
from doing nothing about it for so long
because standing up for my voice always felt so wrong

Solitude

I forced myself into solitude
    Whether I wanted to or not
    It felt safe and comfortable
And no one could disturb my peace
It had nothing to do with the virus looming about
But me wanting to collect myself to reset my mind
Maybe it was unhealthy
But I enjoyed my time with myself
To truly get to know the person I was becoming
And not the person that the world wanted me to be
I may have seemed cold or weary
Maybe even selfish or unkind
But it's something that I had to do in order to move forward
To piece it all together
In a way that makes sense
Without another's opinion of my intentions
It felt right to me and wrong to someone else
But when the time comes and I feel ready I will step out so

everyone knows
   And gets to meet the real me
   I've been slowly building it up and working towards a future
that not everyone can see
   But it doesn't take much just the power to believe

Afraid of It All

Why am I afraid?
What am I afraid of?
The steps I've taken to get here have been different than most, there's been weird detours and strange days of nothing happening

I take the fear and silence as a stepping stone towards the next steps but the way it is fearful

Maybe I am afraid of actually making it somewhere and doing what needs to be done with myself

But my life is my own and I was never meant to follow the crowd but to create my own path in life

I pray for things to change, I beg and I plead but the right moment comes along

and I watch it go away because it all feels too good to be true

and I don't grasp on the things that I know are meant to be mine

but the opportunities come and it feels wrong in some way just because of others stating I should be doing things

differently
    or I should be doing things the more practical way
    but its all just noise
    its all just static in the background of the life that is laid out
for me
    the instructions are planted perfectly where they should be
    this is about me and my own journey through life
    and the stops I've made along the way are just gathering up
the next bit of courage needed
    for the road ahead

Finally Diagnosed

Its like a hurricane constantly inside my brain,
   wanting to do so many things but being frozen solid
   by the fear of possibly not doing enough or doing it
wrong
   so I don't even do it or I hide out and let the days pass me by
   Feeling like a disappointment if I cant get it done
   or the spotlight shines too bright and I go blind
   its a billion tabs open all at once
   not knowing where the music is coming from
   I wrote about it in the last poetry collection
   but back then I didn't know what it was
   I just thought I was crazy,
   society called me lazy
   told me to just pay attention
   but to what do I owe my attention to?
   Now I do and I feel at peace
   knowing there's nothing wrong with me
   Its rolled up in one package like a gift from someone you

don't even want to receive
Jumping from one topic to the next
wondering what word ends up fitting best
its exhausting just sitting there and the thoughts are so loud
and you cant figure out which ones are yours
and which ones are societies
because this world isn't meant for people like us
we are wired for building our own
if only we could get started and stick with it

-ADHD

I Want To Be Free

Underestimation of what I can do
really boils my soul
because I know for sure I am meant
for something so much more than where I am
Where I've been has nothing on where I want to be
High ways and orange leaves on the trees
Stepping into my true destiny
Everyone from before doesn't seem to understand
That I am headed in a different direction
Down a different path
They want me to stay put
But I want to move
I want to be free

Addicted To New Beginnings

f resh starts
   new homes
   new things
new clothes
bored of the old
need to rearrange at least once a month
because I crave new
I can't stay in one place for long
because I never really had one place to call home
four walls and a roof
isn't enough to keep me contained
I have to keep moving
cant settle just yet
cant pursue one career
or program in school
because I want new
but when it came to you
I could never get bored because

you want the same
we both cant stay in the same place for long
and that's why were enough
together

Mountains Inside My Soul

~~~

1ived my life with my eyes closed
not understand why the world was so cruel
tried so hard to make my intentions clear
but i ended up living my life with fear
i know why i am here
its to spread joy and rid the fear
i have to climb the mountains inside my soul
to begin to help make others whole

Frequency Is The Only Way To Go

Perception shifts,
Used to be overwhelming
But now I see it clearly
And everything for what it is
Not what I thought it to be
Ever changing moments
That I didn't give the push too
But fear has trapped my mind
And I was on default mode
But I know the way out
And it's now or never
Never will keep me from seeking
The truth I crave to find
Now will allow things to unfold
The way it's supposed to
I accept all damages
But seek the blessings
It will take some time

And lots of back and forth
But I will get there soon
And keep my mind at the
Frequency of which I plan to go

This Is My Car

t his is the car i am driving
    on this road, we call life
    I may not have a license
but I've been driving blindfolded &
i don't have to pick you up
and let you sit in the passenger seat
do not take control of my steering wheel
or tell me where to go
or I'll be kicking you out
and leaving you to the side of the road
you can hitchhike to where
you wanted me to go
your destination is not my responsibility
my car relies on my ambition
not your decisions
i don't need to drive you around
this is my car not your stomping grounds

This Is My Car

get out and walk
if you can't handle where im headed
my life isn't based on your direction

Learning To Live Again

I struggle sometimes, just because the trauma part of my brain tells me what I'm doing is not important and I should be doing something more practical with my time... But I start to really think that through and realize maybe not many are watching but I know my purpose in life is something much bigger than what I've been used to my entire life.

& Literally, every day since I started this journey teaches me something new, no matter how painful the blow may be the realization that comes afterwards is uncomfortable but important. When I said I was going through a healing journey I wasn't joking with you, I was literally pushing myself through hell and back and so many days and nights of raging confusion just to get to somewhere beautiful that I didn't think existed...

I'm, not the same person who started this journey, even if sometimes there's a step back to take. I am only human and sometimes my mind needs to catch up with everything going on and it gets overwhelming and I can't believe I've made it this far.

Until I started catching glimpses of it and actually following the path that it's leading me to, this is a never-ending journey that's not going to stop until I learn the lessons meant to be learned. I've had to make a lot of sacrifices this year, things that may not be huge to you or someone going through more than I am but enough that it broke me down for a while but no matter what I always seem to find a light somewhere during the storm. I keep stopping and starting projects because I feel like they aren't important enough to make a difference but I've spent the last few months planting the seeds and now I'm ready to watch them grow.

Even when someday I don't know what I'm doing or what my purpose even is...

Our struggles are not a competition with one another, everyone journeys through life differently and each different story should have its own support, I'm not perfect and don't ever think I could be but my mindset has come a long way and I don't think I could ever look back.

Little Ol' Me

d ear little ol me
    how have you been
    it's been years since
I don't know when
I know you're still watching
I know you're still there
I know you think
that people don't care
your light shined bright on so many dark souls
maybe you were
all they came to know
the ones that hurt and the ones that fought
didn't think they'd realize what they have lost
you are safe and you are alright
it is time for you to stop the fight
I've got it from here
you may now rest
little old me,

you've passed the test

How Did I Get Here?

W hat a crazy year its been?
        Felt like ive been wandering since,
        I dont know when.
Its almost over
and we are almost threw
so many lessons learned
so many mistakes I cant undo
The battle was treacherous
and the mountain was high
but I've learned
theirs nothing i cannot climb
I finally feel free
I finally am where
Ive always dreamt I would be
Never wanting to go back
to the places that I have been
and the things that I have seen
all of those memories

felt oh so mean
and the people ive met
and the battles they've fought
I will keep to myself
All that they have taught
Every road leads to somewhere new
even the ones that you had to battle
your way through
The warrior I am
and the woman I will be
Will give thanks to everything
That I thought would end me

A Journey

i 've set off on a journey
one others continue to doubt
i follow my intuition
and go to where my soul knows
but if im not making any money
they won't leave me alone
and say that i failed
walking away and making my own trail
paving my own road
and carrying everyone elses load
i know what i want
and i know what im after

Climbing This Mountain

i have been working so hard
   and pushing on through
   just so focused
on what i need to do
fighting against
what society wants me to do
i need to center my focus &
remove the distractions
so i can focus on climbing this mountain

Stories Meant To Be Told

he calm before the storm came to pass, and I knew the feeling wasn't going to last.

But I speak my truth and say what I mean, I mean what I say and do not take it back.

The storm hit me, and I nearly drowned, I wanted to let it take me from here.

To a place I knew only existed if you had let it be so.

But I will not let it be so, the storm passed and now its time to share.

To share what struck me down, but also what woke me up and carried me to where im supposed to be.

Back onto the path of the great unknown, to tell the stories meant to be told.

Trust The Process

Trust the process
    Nothing makes sense right now
    But soon it will
And the struggle will be understood
And you will be able to step
Forward in faith not fear
And forget about those you've lost
Who you've truely loved dear
Even if they have questions
Tell them to trust the process
Things will happen naturally
And things will grow
The way it's supposed to
Don't ask questions
Let it happen the way
You feel is right

Revolving Door

The world is exhausting
  When you feel like time is running out
  And you're not sure what for
But it feels like a revolving door
And you can't find a spot to sit
And everyone around you doesn't seem to understand
They're stuck in there ways of living when everything is
clearly different
  we need to stop acting like everything is the same because its
not
  the world is undergoing so many different changes
  and so is our minds
  now we need to change our attitudes towards the future
  and make the changes needed to better the future and
understand that
  not everyone is walking the same path as the rest of the world
  some are paving their own road
  its going to take some time to get there

but when we get there it will be beautiful
and everyones world will be spun upside down
its time for me to step out of the shadows
and take a leap to the unknown
providing for anyone
willing to wait for
the results to be shown

I Choose The Light

How long have I been asleep for?
I ask the universe as I open my eyes to a
Bright new world I'm surrounded by
The sun is so many different shades of red as it sets
And the grass is so green and feels like its growing beneath
your feet
Am I supposed to be here?
I ask and the universe points towards the door behind me
labeled
"the other you"
And flashes of going no where and accomplishing nothing
fill my mind
And I say no thank you I'll choose the light

Safe Mindset

When you've lived most of your life in one mindset
one that is safe,
it makes it hard to improve your life
at everyone else pace
they ask, why can't you just get better
and I want to but my mind is like a prison
and it has thrown away the key in every attempt I've made
has me falling apart at the scenes
think I've recovered only to fall back apart
trying to find myself back at the start

The Memories

The memories make me sick to my stomach
     & they probably always will.
         Witnessing things that weren't meant to happen,
Things I should have said
didn't clue in until the end
Knowing the behavior was unacceptable
But allowing it to continue for so long
Is a guilt I have to hold onto
Even though its not something I want to
I try not to think of it as time wasted
But lessons learned to move on from
Knowing one-day karma will catch up to you
I will move on but I will never forget
But the scars will one day heal
and the pain won't always feel this real

Life I am Aiming For

A lot of people doubt because the path I'm taking isn't conventional. It's a path my soul chooses, and in order to get there, I have to define the odds. Not "prove people wrong" but fight against what is seen as normal or accepted by society.

My life feels like there are two roads, one road full of people doing life the way it's supposed to be, following the rules, and accepting society's expectations.

And then the other road, everyone's doing one way and I'm going against the natural flow.

I was not destined to live a typical lifestyle
my life is not meant to be silent
I am supposed to be loud
even if people disagree with me
I am supposed to fall

because I will always rise
nothing in this world makes sense anymore
and if everyone were to open their eyes and see this
the world would be a much different place
but so many are stuck in their ways
and there's not much we can do to change their minds
except for focusing on our own path and if they follow
be there to guide and support but if they don't
I am awakened to the truth
of what not many seem to know of
they're all asleep and set in their ways
even though my mind is programmed to go against it
I will fight for the life I am aiming for

Borrowed Moments

Time doesn't feel like time when
You're living on borrowed moments
In memory of the me that used to be and no longer
is
I don't function at that frequency anymore it's all a mask
That I'm pretending to wear that I can't take off
Because society is fucked and makes us into someone we
aren't
In order to be able to play the part
Until the certain closes
How am I the only one who can see all this?
It's not only depressing it's moronic
And repetitive
But I feel guilty wanting to leave it because the ones I love
are living it
But me, I can't do it anymore without spacing out and day
dreaming
And begging reality to catch up with the thoughts that come

in

Despite the logic of those who are stuck and only take a vacation in the summer

But I want to work so hard and build my dream world without the guilt

So I don't have to live for the weekend and be able to help others discover this about themselves

Years and years I believed this was the only way to do this road called life, and maybe to them it is

But I know I'm personally meant for so much more even though my time in that perspective is coming to an end

And it all makes sense at some point

But is what I'm feeling truly real, or am I just the type that all she does is feel?

You Will Make It Out Of This

its fighting a war in side your mind
from who you were to where you are to where you wanna be
its having to take a break for a day from all your goals and ambitions
because your mind is at a constant war of doubt and becoming so far behind
that you dont even feel its worth it to get up and continue
its days of ecstasy and bliss getting so much done
but also wondering if its even enough
its wondering how it even got so bad in the first place
and bills being piled up
but not knowing how to take care of them
its frustrating and lonely
but the first step of healing
truly is knowing
and being aware that the patterns before
were not meant for you to grow

and being that person who
was too afraid to even move
because you never bothered to figure it out to begin with
its loving life one day and wondering when its going
to finally end the next day
days of making plans and many of not following through
losing people who cant seem to understand
even tho you're trying so hard to d
you know it will get better
you just aren't sure when
so its putting on a brave face
and pushing through the day
and fighting to get out of bed
being stuck in your head
nothing makes sense
everyone thinks you're just dense
but thats not true
you've just been stuck feeling blue
and you will be alright
and make it out of this
-SC

Have No Fear

t his book needs to end here
but have no fear, my dear
give me another year or two
to follow my wildest dreams
and I will be back writing another three
about the next journeys life will allow me to take
I will leave it up to the hands of fate
hopefully less heartbreak
and more insane stories to tell
and reunited with a lost love
who knows what the title will be
but you may have to wait another year or three
hopefully, I won't procrastinate
and the book won't come out too late
but it been fun
here's to more stories that have just begun

Friends With My Shadows

You threw me down to rock bottom,
    Thinking I'd lay down and let you win,
    thought I'd let you get away with the damage caused
Assumed I'd retaliate and cause a riot
But I built a home down there,
I became friends with my shadow while you still battle with
yours
    While I walked around on eggshells trying not to anger
The monster within you
You danced freely and laughed as I walked away
Thinking you had won and I'd come back for more
But no,
The window-shattering scream I let out
Freed myself from your grasp
Don't think I don't know what your intentions were
Because I may be quiet, and I may be polite
But I am not stupid and I'm not afraid to release
What I've been holding back

You, on the other hand, don't care who you hurt
As long you look innocent in the end
Your minions will figure it out in time
Until then, I will walk with my head held high
Letting the damage within you
Dance with the devil

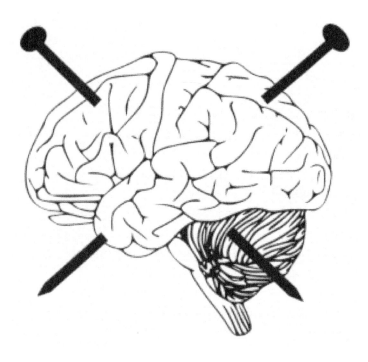

Going Forward

Now I have a better idea of the path ahead
   I'll try not to spend so much time in my head
   Reflected on what I survived
   When they thought I wouldn't make it through
   the traps they had set
   But here I am taking a new approach to life
   turning what I thought would kill me into
   a survival guide for others doing the same
   To let someone else know they aren't alone on this road
   Going forward speaking my mind and raising my voice
   If someone has to go I will hold the door open for them
   I know what is right and what has a red flags to it
   I am the creator of my future
   Going forward the poetry will be less on dark matters
   and more of the beauty I will experience
   Not turning back to feel the hurt
   But remember that I made it through that
   I will make it through anything that comes my way

Printed in Great Britain
by Amazon